Pips Prank

by Tim Little
Illustrated by Bill Ledger

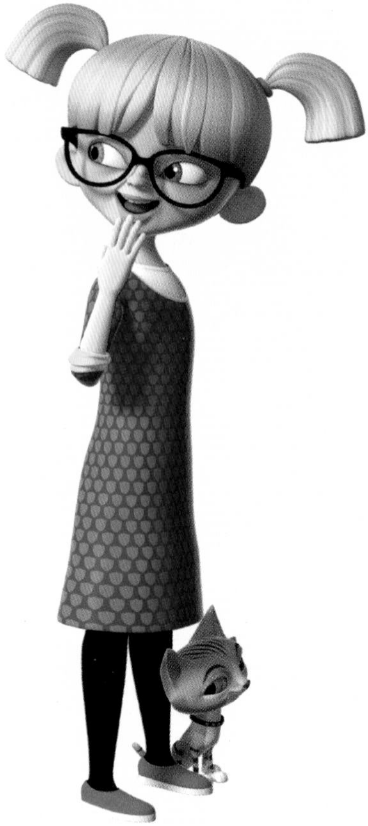

OXFORD
UNIVERSITY PRESS

In this story ...

Pip

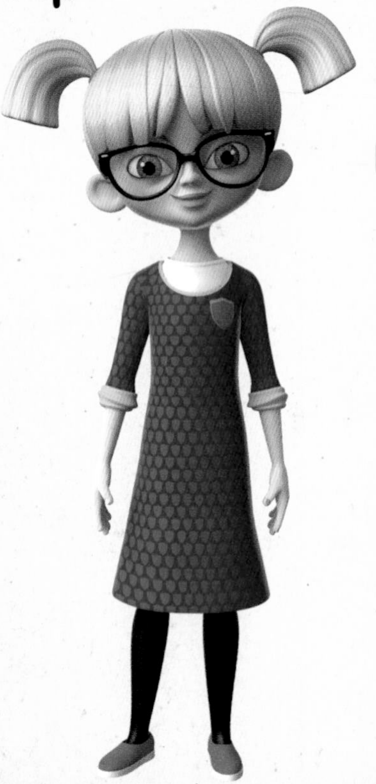

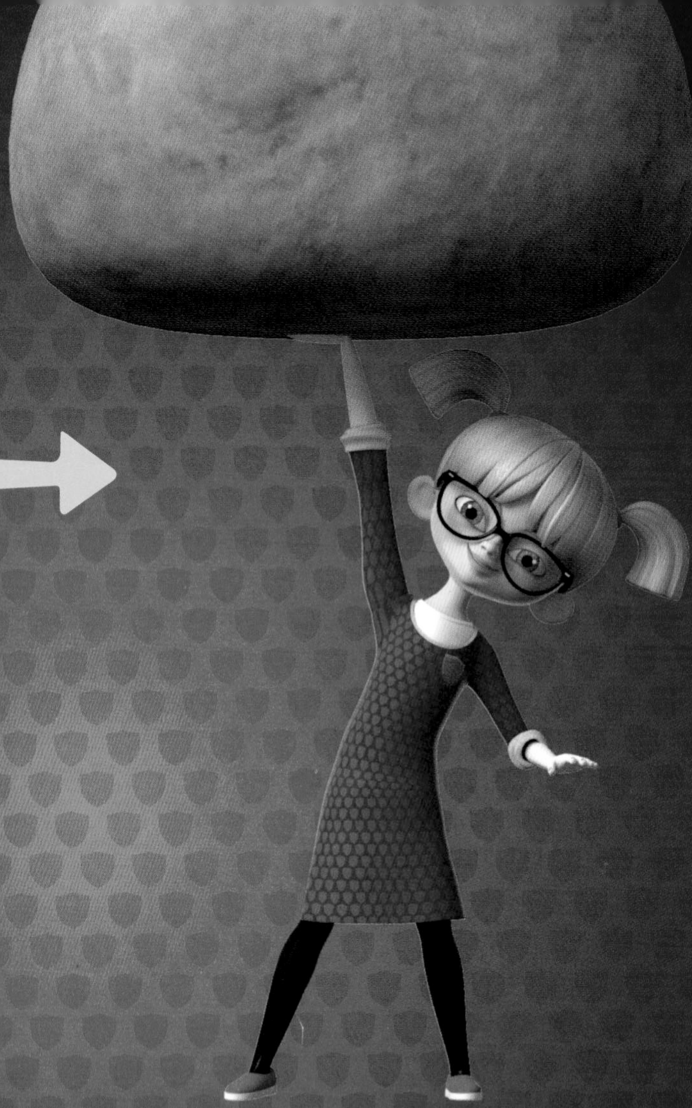

Ben

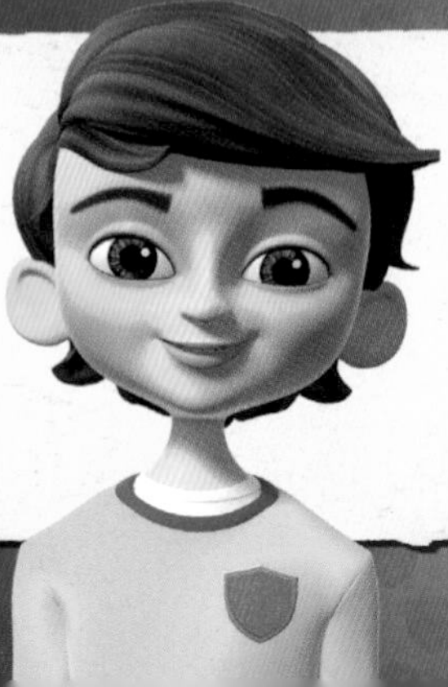

Slink

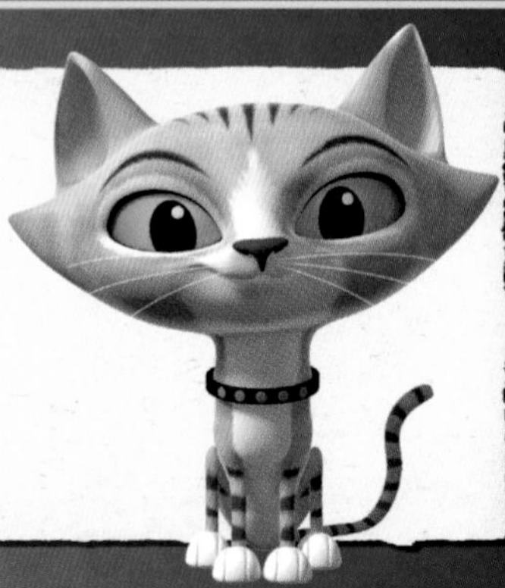

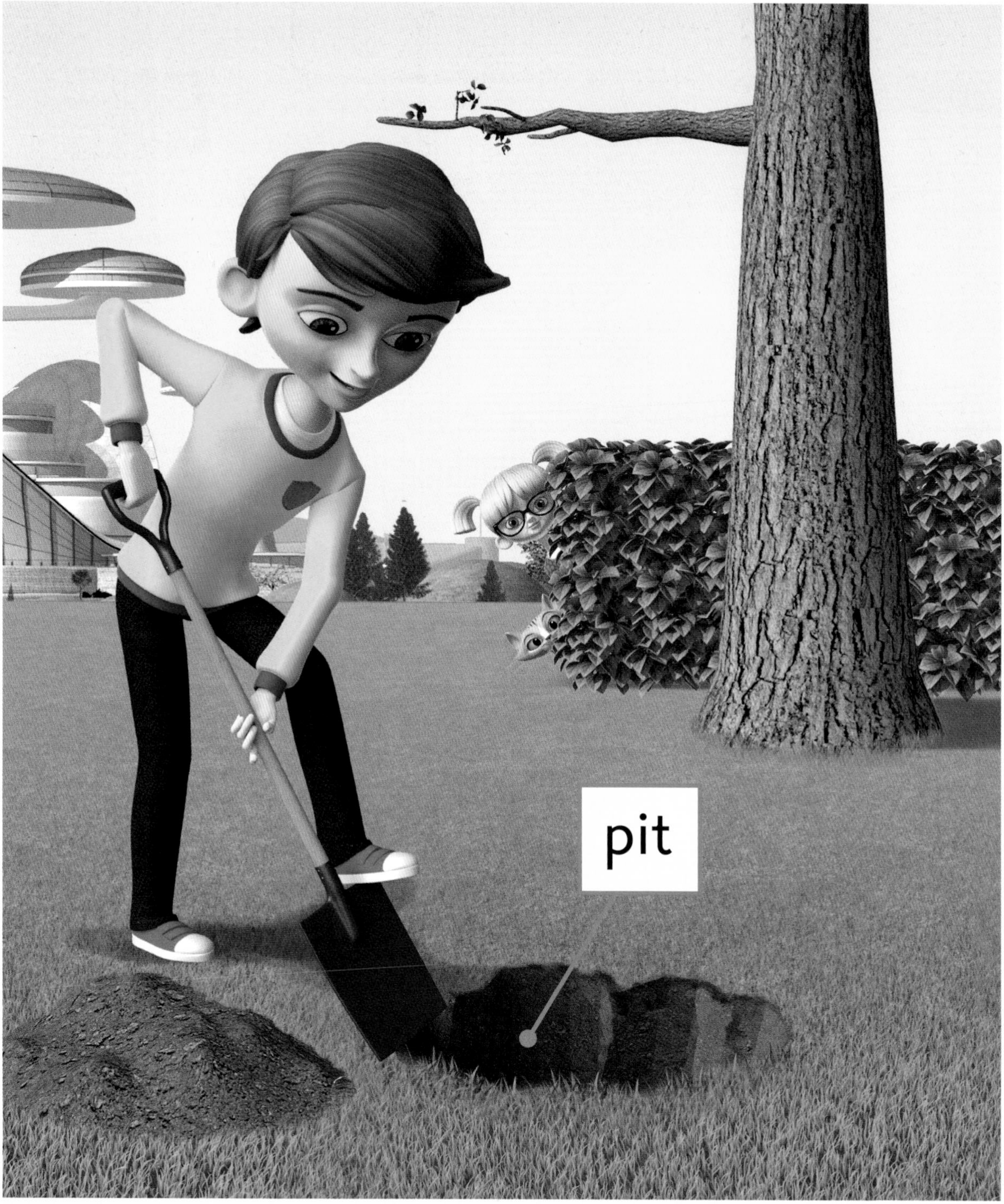
pit

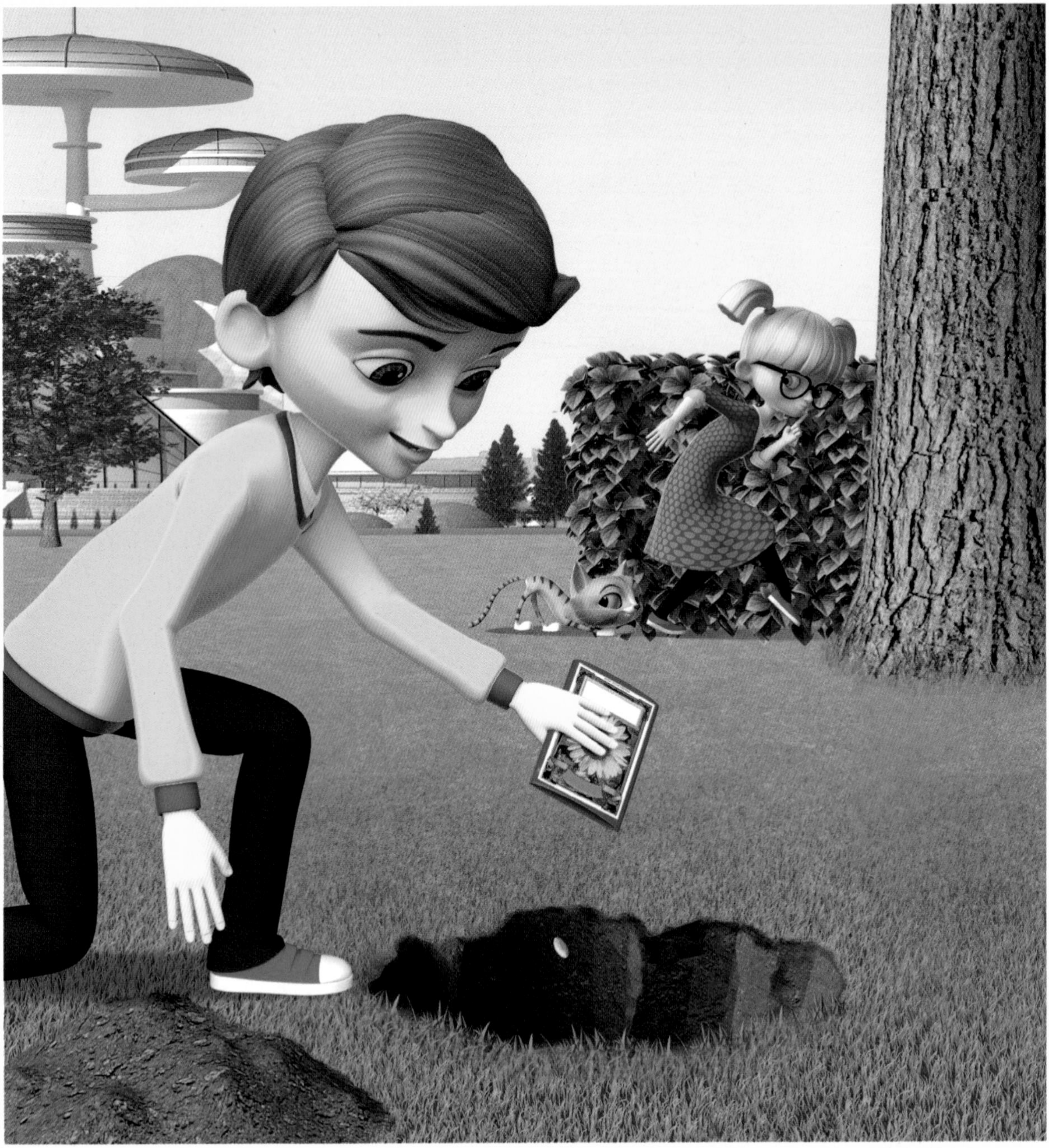

Ben tips it in.

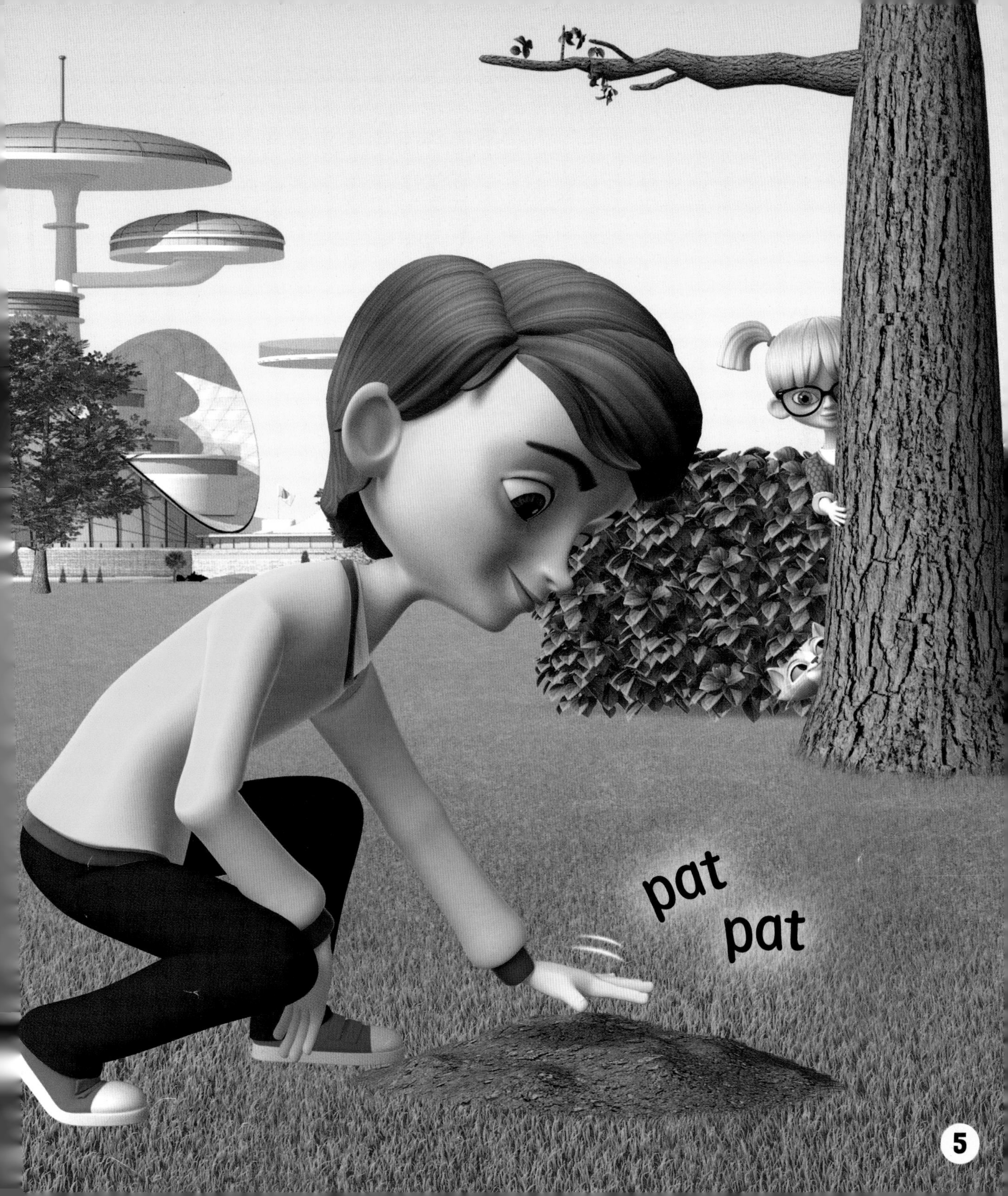
pat
pat

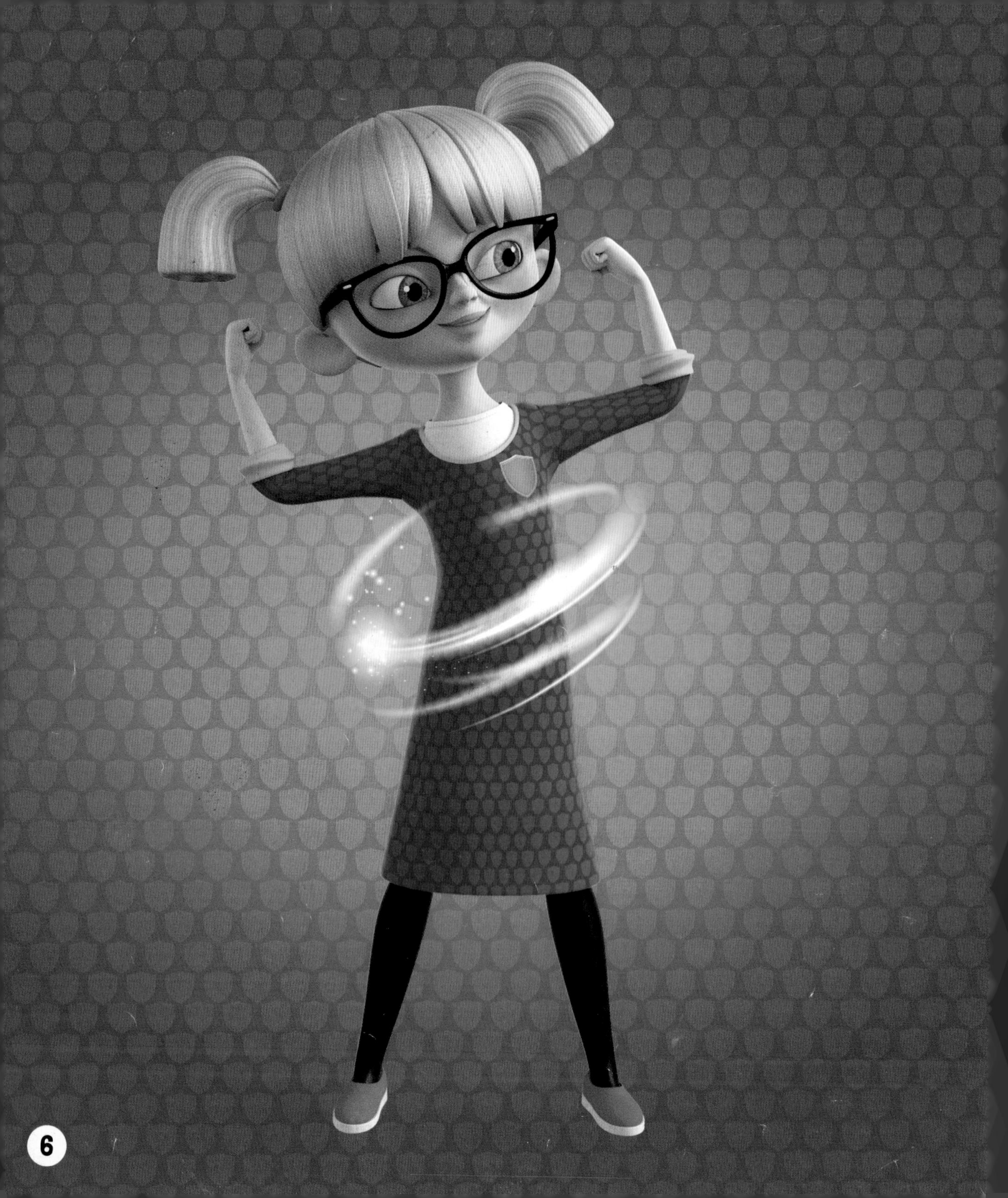

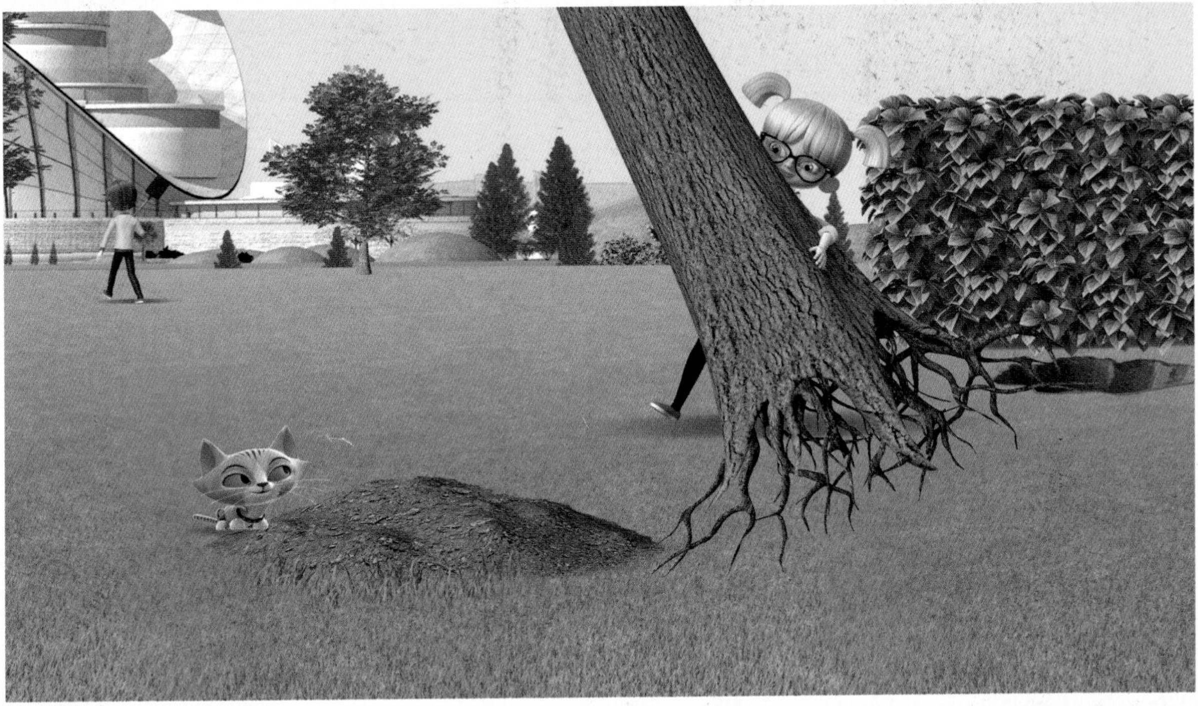

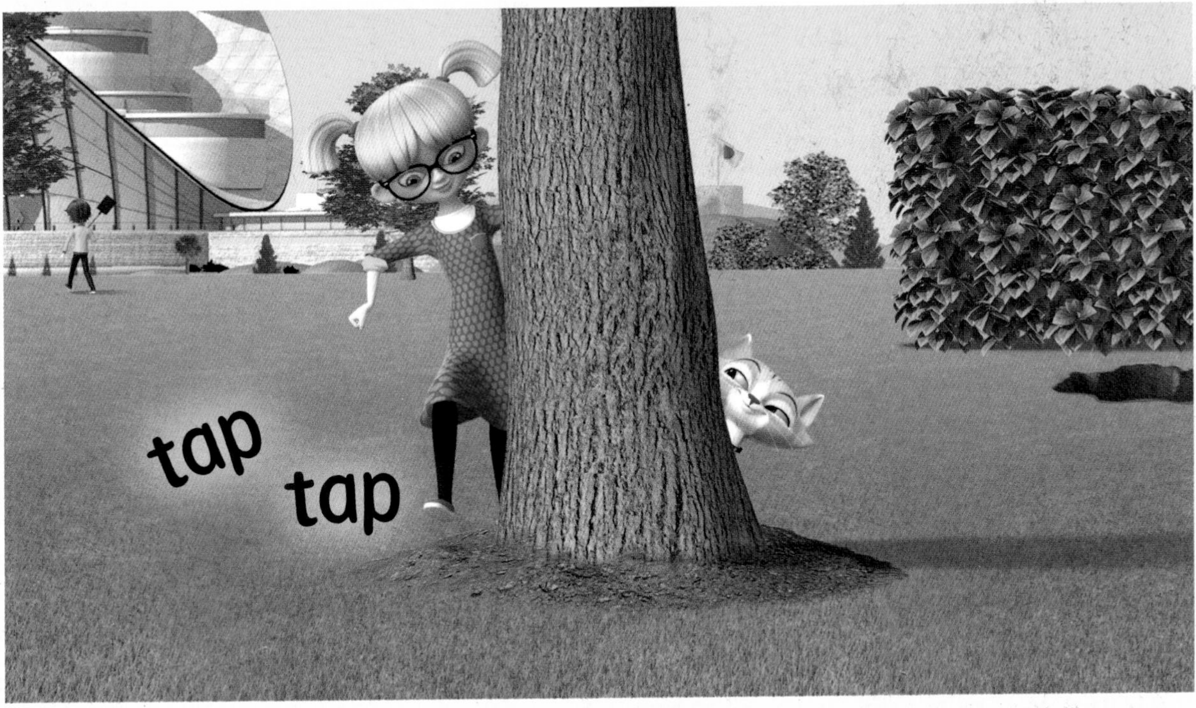
tap
tap

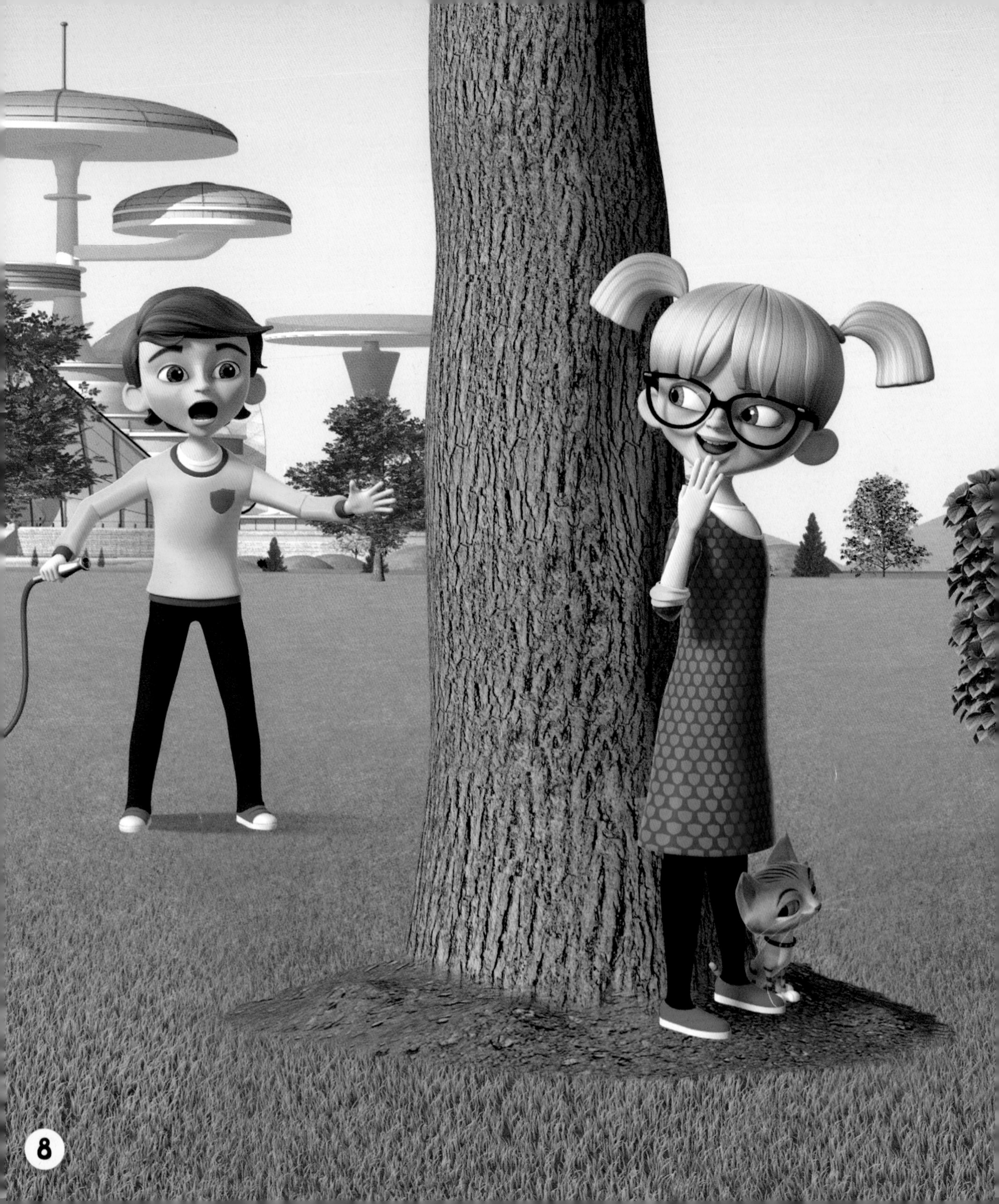

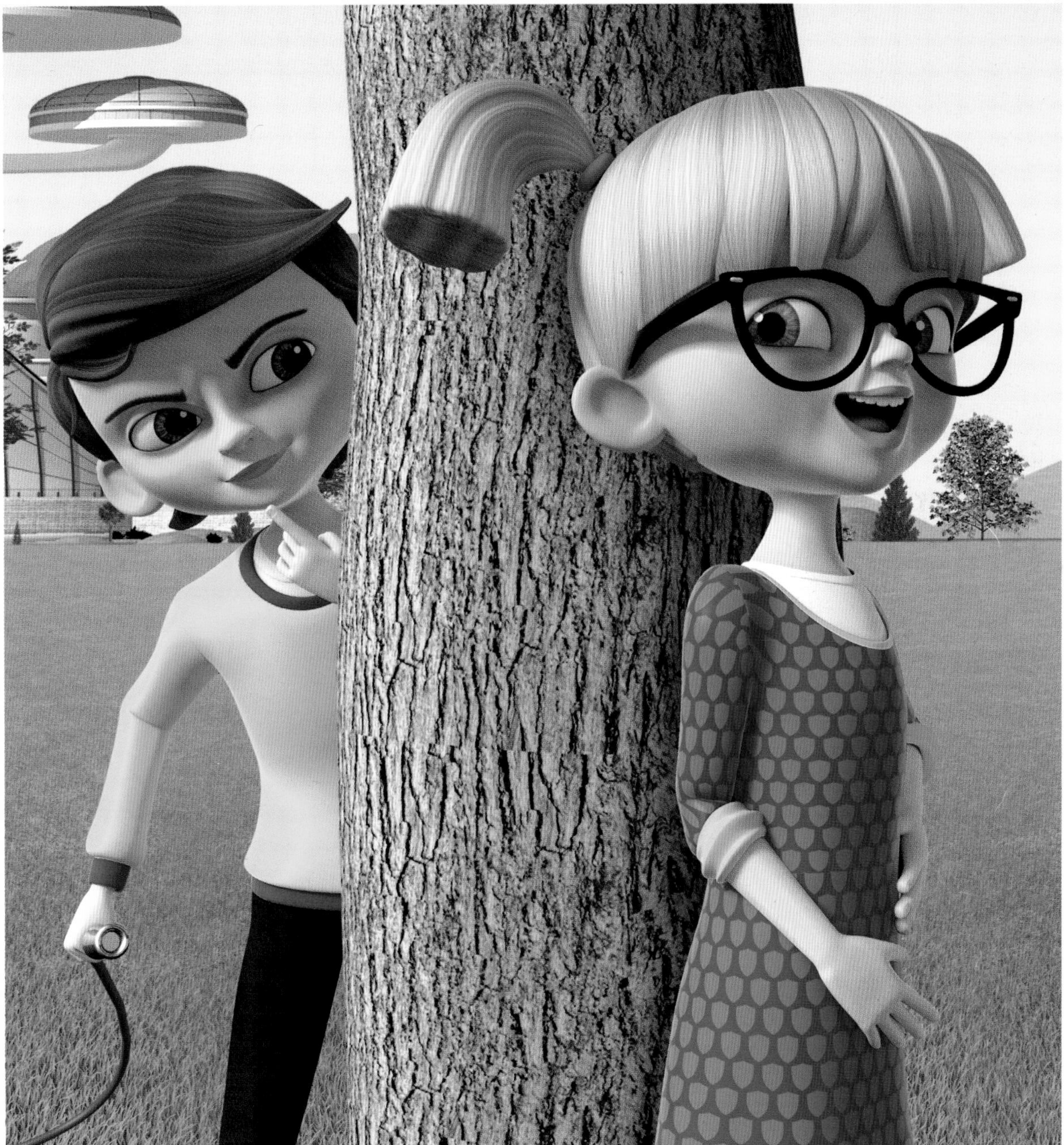

Ben is mad.

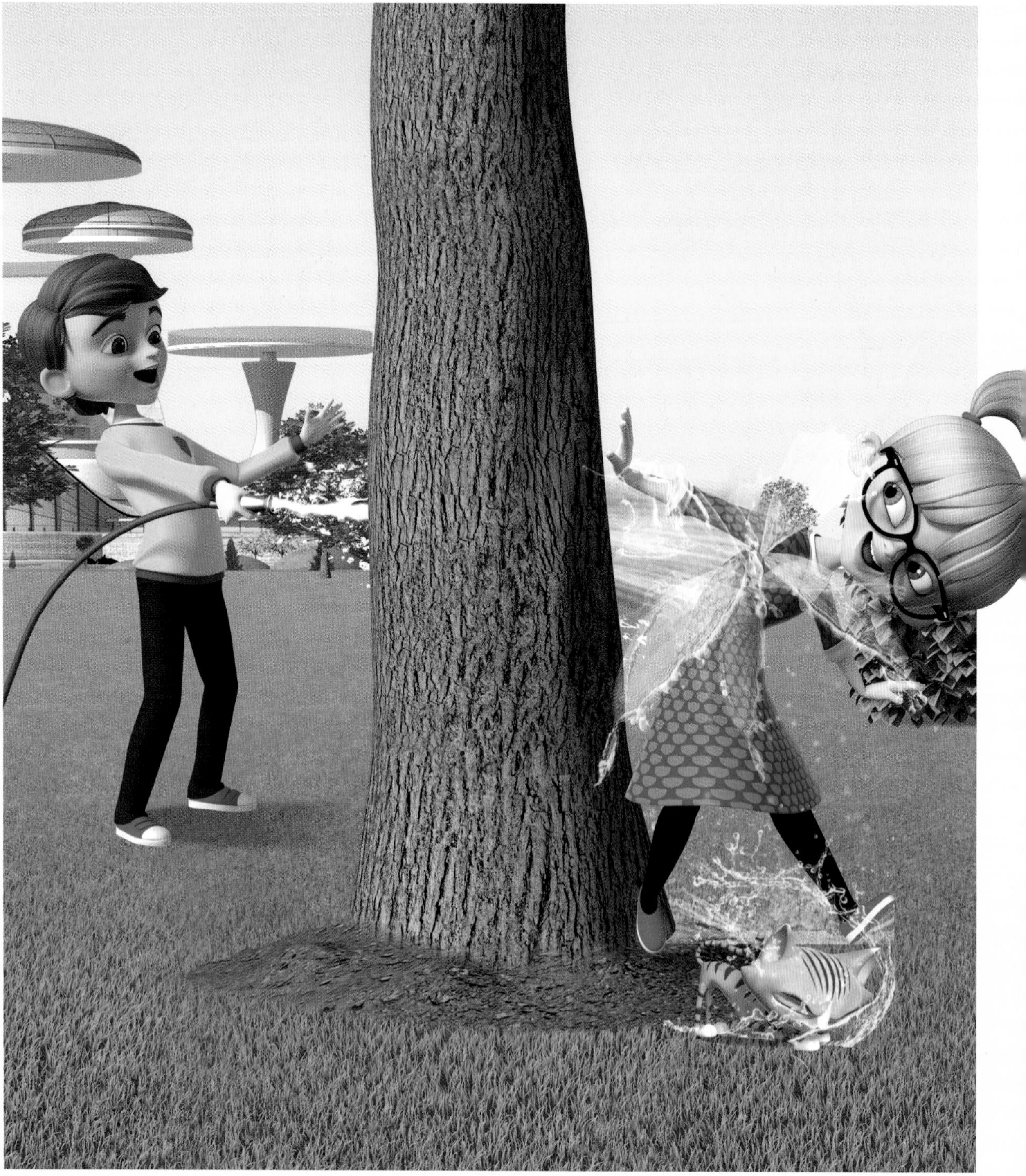

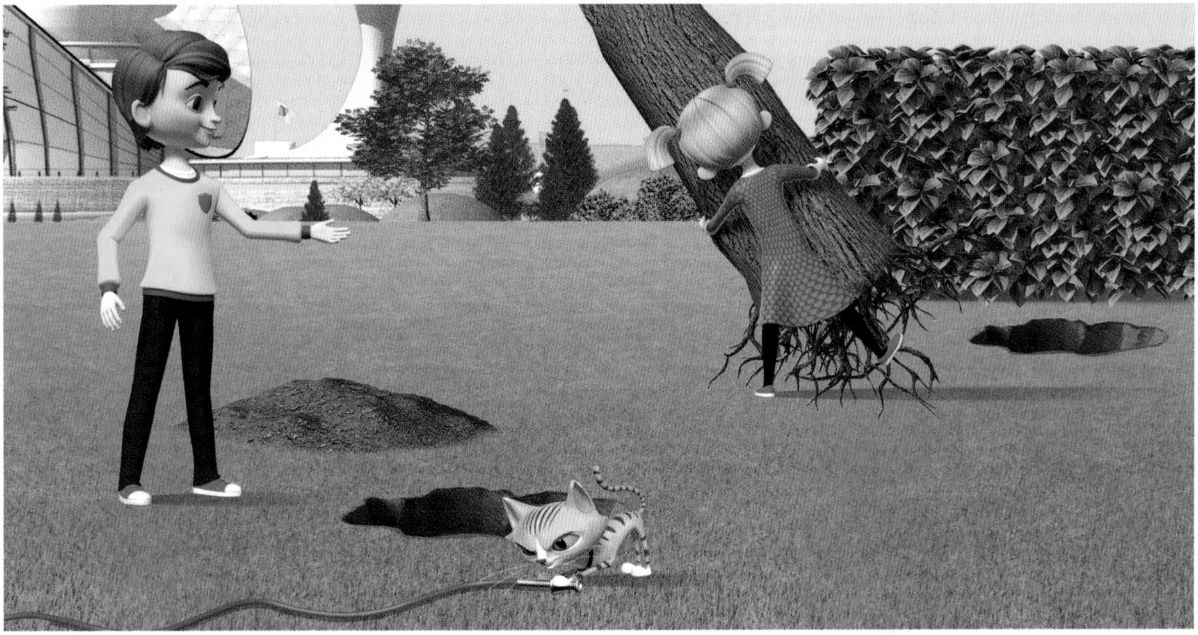

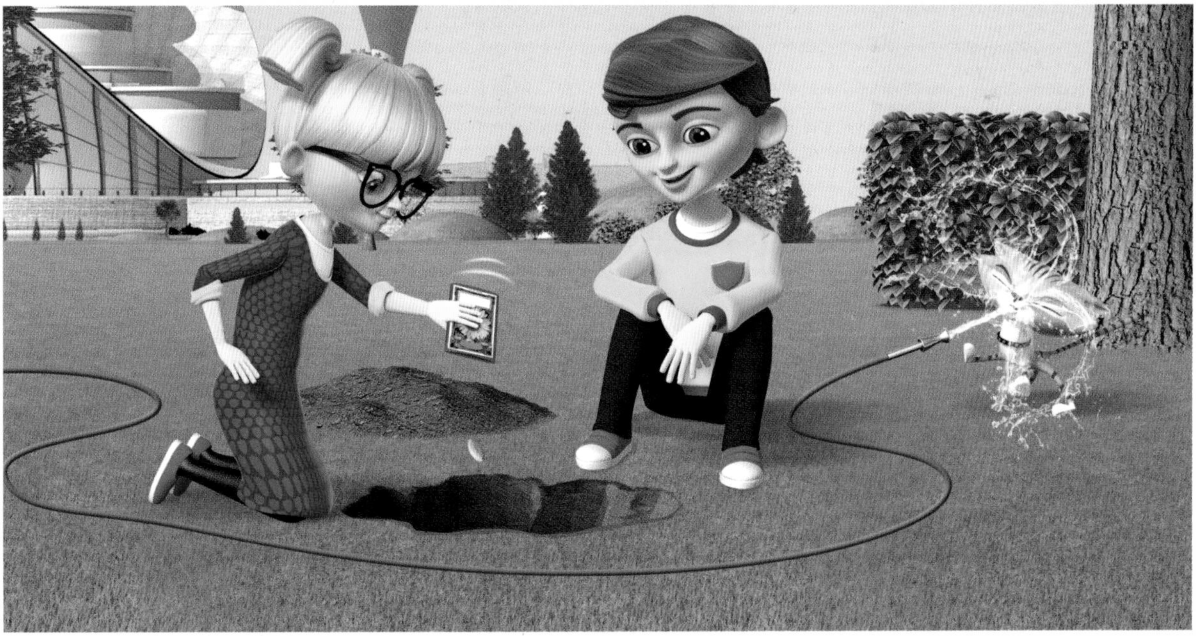

Pip and Ben sit.

Retell the story ...

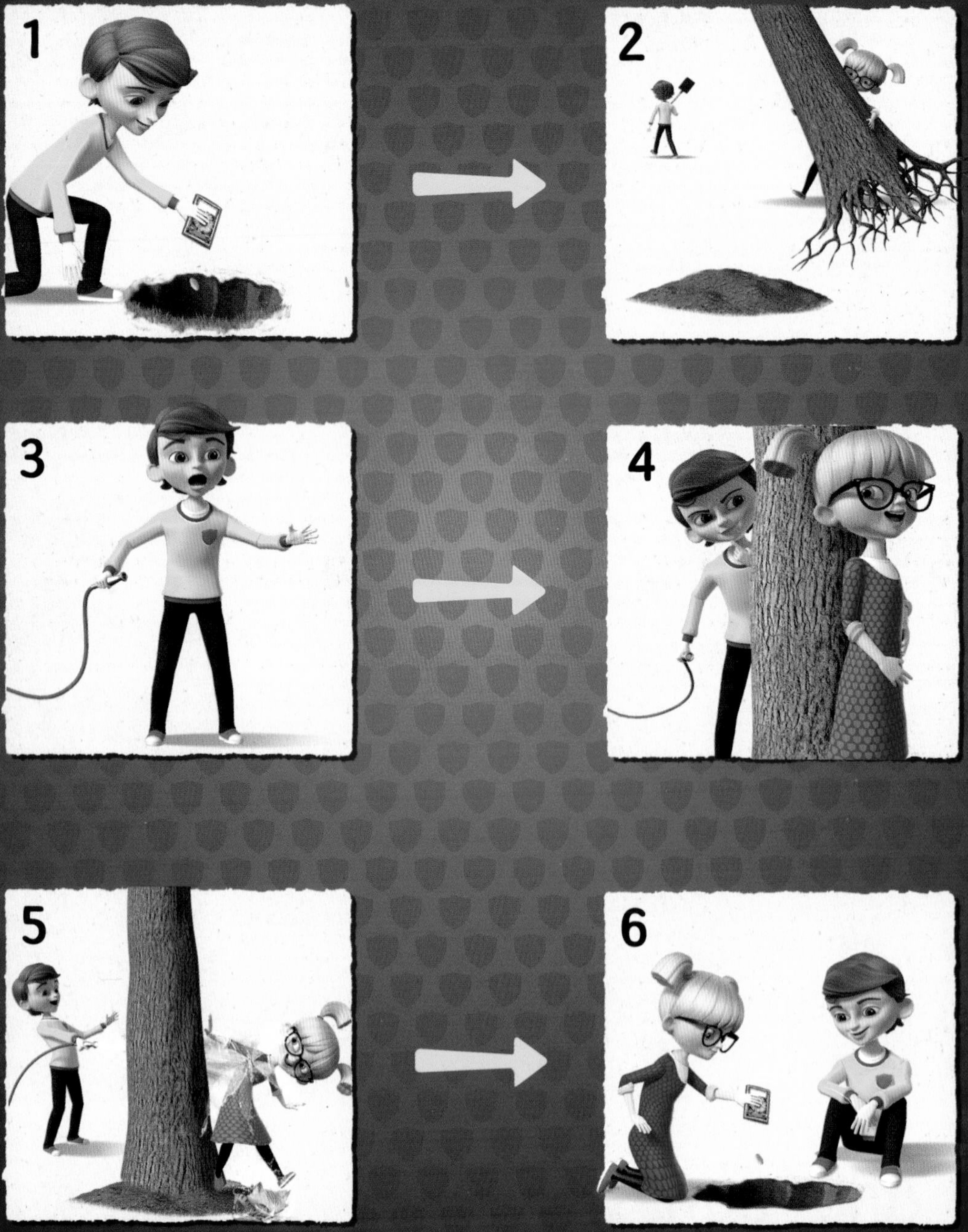